MY WORLD OF SCIENCE

Forces and Motion

Revised and Updated

Angela Royston

Heinemann Library
Chicago, Illinois

Customer Service 888-454-2279
Visit our website at www.heinemannraintree.com

Design: Joanna Hinton-Malivoire
Printed in the United States of America in North Mankato, Minnestoa. 082012   006898

14 13 12
10 9 8 7 6 5 4 3 2 1

New edition ISBN-13:   978-1-4329-1433-2 (hardcover)
                           978-1-4329-1455-4 (paperback)
            ISBN-10:   1-4329-1433-2 (hardcover)
                           1-4329-1455-3 (paperback)

The Library of Congress has cataloged the first edition as follows:
Royston, Angela
  Forces and motion/ Angela Royston.
    p. cm. --(My world of science)
  Includes bibliographic references and index.
  ISBN 1-58810-240-8
  1. Force and energy – Juvenile literature 2. Motion
  – Juvenile literature. [1. Force and energy. 2. Motion.] I. Title.
  QC73.4 .R69 2001

531'.6--dc21

Acknowledgements
The publishers would like to thank the following for permission to reproduce photographs: © Alamy/ Arco Images p. 19; © Bubbles p. 26 (Frans Rombout); © Corbis pp. 8, 11, 16, 20 (Henrykk Trigg), 28, 29; © Powerstock Zefa p. 10; © Robert Harding p. 5; © Science Photo Library pp. 6 (Dr Marley Read), 7 (Maximillian Stock); © Stone pp. 8, 12, 13; © Trevor Clifford pp. 14, 15, 17, 18, 21, 22, 23, 24, 25; © Trip pp. 4 (H. Rogers), 27 (P. Aikman).

Cover photograph reproduced with permission of © Getty Images/Wild Pics.

The publishers would like to thank Jon Bliss for his assistance in the preparation of this book.

Every effort has been made to contact copyright holders of any material reproduced in this book. Any omissions will be rectified in subsequent printings if notice is given to the publishers.

Contents

Any words appearing in the text in bold, **like this**, are explained in the glossary.

What Is a Force?

A force makes things move. These people are moving a piano. One man is pushing it. The other man is pulling it.

Pulls and pushes are forces. This rider is pushing down on the pedals to make the bicycle wheels move forward.

Machines and Forces

This bulldozer is pushing earth and trees out of the way. Machines have **engines** that make the force to move heavy loads.

jib

cable

This crane is lifting a heavy load. The engine makes a force that moves the jib. The jib pulls up the cable and the cable pulls up the load.

Natural Forces

Wind and moving water are powerful **natural** forces. Wind is air that is moving. It can bend trees and push leaves through the air.

Moving water also pushes things. This boat is floating down a river. The moving water is a force that pushes the boat.

Moving Your Body

We use our **muscles** to make our body move. Muscles can push and pull the different parts of our body.

This climber is pushing and pulling herself up a steep rock.

You can move in many different ways. This woman is swimming. The muscles in her arms, legs, and feet make a force that moves her through the water.

Stopping

Forces can also be used to stop something moving. This dog wants to move forward. But its owner is pulling it backwards, to stop it.

Pushing or pulling against something that is moving can slow it down or stop it. The players in yellow are pulling the player in white. They are trying to stop him.

Changing Shape

Forces can be used to make some things change shape. It is easy to pull and push soft clay into many different shapes.

This boy is squeezing an empty carton to push the air out. This will make the carton flatter and smaller, so it will take up less space in the trash can.

Squeezing an empty carton pushes the air out of it.

Changing Direction

Forces can make something change direction. This tennis player is pushing his racket against the ball. The ball changes direction and goes back across the net.

Forces can also make something turn in a circle. You have to twist the top of a jar one way to get it off. You twist it the other way to put the top on.

Getting Faster

The harder you push something, the faster it moves. This girl is pushing a toy train across the floor. If she gives it a big push, it will move faster.

This **athlete** is working hard to jump as far as he can. He pushes his feet down and backward on the ground to move himself up and forward.

Slopes

A **slope** can change how fast something moves. This person is skiing down a slope. The **steeper** the slope, the faster the skier will move.

This woman is pushing her wheelbarrow up a slope. Pushing up a slope is harder than pushing on flat ground.

Friction

Friction is a force that slows things down. This boy is pushing his toy and then letting go. The toy moves quickly at first, then it slows down and stops.

The toy slows down because its wheels rub against the ground. The rubbing is called friction. **Rough** wheels cause more friction than smooth wheels.

Testing Friction

This boy is using balls and a **ramp** to test which kind of floor has the most **friction** – carpet or wood. He measures how far the ball rolls.

carpet

ramp

The carpet is **rough** and the wood is smooth. Does the ball roll further on the carpet or on the wood? (Answer on page 31.)

wood

Using Friction

People can use **friction** to slow themselves down. When children push their arms and feet against the sides of a slide, the friction will slow them down.

This boy's hands will get warm as he pushes because friction creates heat.

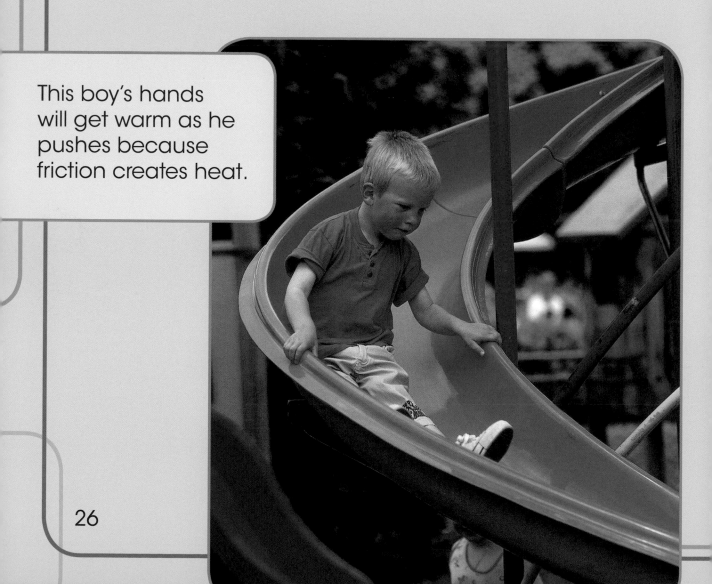

Bicycle brakes use friction to slow down. When you pull the brake handle, two rubber blocks grip against the wheel. This stops the wheel from moving as freely.

brake block

More and Less Friction

The **soles** of your shoes are **rough**. They create **friction** between your feet and the ground. Friction stops you from slipping when you move your feet.

Some soles have a pattern to create even more friction.

The less friction there is, the more you slide. Snow is very smooth, so there is very little friction. Skiers slide fast across the slippery snow.

Glossary

athlete person who takes part in a running, jumping, or throwing sport

engine something that uses electricity or fuel, such as gasoline or diesel, to make a machine move

friction rubbing between one object and another that slows movement down

muscle part of your body that helps you move

natural something made by nature, not by people or machines

ramp something used to make a slope

rough bumpy or uneven

slope surface that goes upward or downward

sole bottom of a shoe

steep when a slope goes up or down very sharply

Answer

Page 25—The ball has rolled farther on wood than on carpet, showing that there is less friction between the ball and the wood.

More Books to Read

Hewitt, Sally. *Amazing Science: Forces and Movement.* London, UK: Hodder Wayland, 2006.

Llewellyn, Claire. *Start-Up Science: Forces and Movement.* London, UK: Evans Brothers, Ltd, 2004.

Sadler, Wendy. *Science in Your Life – Forces: The ups and downs.* Chicago: Raintree, 2005.

Index